Electricity and the Lightbulb

GREAT INVENTIONS

Electricity and the Lightbulb

JAMES LINCOLN COLLIER

Marshall Cavendish
Benchmark
New York

Marshall Cavendish Benchmark
99 White Plains Road
Tarrytown, NY 10591-9001
www.marshallcavendish.us

Library of Congress Cataloging-in-Publication Data

Collier, James Lincoln, 1928–
Electricity and the lightbulb / James Lincoln Collier.
p. cm. — (Great inventions)
ISBN 0-7614-1878-4
1. Lightbulbs. [1. Electric lighting.] I. Title. II. Series.

TK4351.C65 2005
621.32—dc22
2004021623

Series design by Sonia Chaghatzbanian

Photo research by Candlepants, Inc.

Cover photo: Randy Faris/Corbis

The photographs in this book are used by permission and through the courtesy of: *Corbis:* 11;
Bettmann, 2,13, 15, 16, 18, 19, 31, 34, 36, 40, 44, 46, 50, 56, 66, 70, 71, 73, 74, 77, 84–85; Steve
Prezant, 8; Gary Bartholomew, 28, 90–91; Stefano Bianchetti, 42–43, 51; Burstein Collection, 48;
Werner H. Muller, 54; Hulton-Deutsch Collection, 60; Christie's Images, 62; Museum of the City of
New York, 80; Tom Wagner/SABA, 88. *John Jenkins/www.sparksmuseum.com:* 21, 24–25, 30, 83.
Getty Images: Time Life Pictures, 64; Hulton Archive, 68, 78.

Printed in China

1 3 5 6 4 2

CONTENTS

Electricity and the Lightbulb

Even the simplest of tasks in our everyday lives is often aided by electricity. Not long ago the "all-electric kitchen" was a novelty; today, anything else would be unthinkable.

ONE

Science Is Born

It is difficult to imagine life today without electricity. Almost every minute of every day this silent force is serving us. Consider an average morning for an ordinary citizen—let us call her Jane Doe. Jane is awakened in the morning by an electric alarm clock, then takes a shower using water heated by electricity and driven through pipes by an electric pump. Jane puts on a skirt and a blouse that have been laundered in an electrically powered washer and dryer. She goes to the kitchen and takes a bottle of orange juice from an electric refrigerator, then pours a cup of coffee from a machine that has been programmed by electricity to have the coffee ready at eight o'clock. She toasts a bagel in an electric toaster, and while she is eating her breakfast watches the morning news on a television set that uses electricity to convert electromagnetic waves to visual images. When Jane has finished breakfast, she hastily sticks the dirty dishes into an electric dishwasher.

Jane then goes to the garage, where she punches a button to open the garage door automatically, starts her car with an electric battery, and sets off for work, getting weather and traffic reports on a radio operated by electricity. As she drives, electrically controlled flashing signs warn her of construction on the road ahead.

At work, Jane reaches her office floor in an elevator run by electricity and turns on the electric lights in her cubicle. She sits in her chair and begins working on her computer—run, of course, by electricity.

And this is only a part of it, for all around her, far and near, electrically driven devices are seeing to it that the world she lives in runs in an efficient and orderly way. Subways and commuter trains, propelled by electric motors, bring her co-workers to the office. Airplanes, guided by a complex array of electric controls, bring needed supplies to the company she works for. In recording studios, engineers are readying the entertainment, consisting of electrical sounds and sights, that Jane will enjoy that evening. And in nearby factories, machines driven by electric motors are turning out the necessities and luxuries that have come to be so much a part of society. Truly, Jane's world runs on electricity.

We take this strange "power" so much for granted that we forget how critical it is to our lives—until a blackout occurs and the world around us ceases to run. Nor do we realize how new this world really is. The grandparents of some of today's students once lived in houses without electricity. In those homes, clocks and watches had to be wound regularly, food was stored in iceboxes chilled by chunks of ice delivered two or three times a week, and clothes were washed in tubs by hand and dried in the sun on clotheslines, even in winter. For children growing up in these homes, there was no radio, no television, and no computer games. On holidays they had no motorboats and no snowmobiles. They walked or rode bicycles to school rather than traveling in the comfort of a bus and in winter bundled up in heavy sweaters in classrooms heated by coal stoves.

Without electricity, the world was a much different place. There were some advantages, of course: the air and lakes were cleaner, the days and nights quieter. But it was certainly a less comfortable and less efficient way of living. The arrival of the electric world about a hundred years ago was one of the major events of the modern industrial age, and it came with a startling suddenness.

The development of electricity is really several stories. First, human

ICEBOXES WERE ONCE COOLED BY REAL ICE, BROUGHT BY AN ICE MAN WHO DELIVERED IT REGULARLY SEVERAL TIMES A WEEK. THE ELECTRIC REVOLUTION CAME WITH ASTONISHING SWIFTNESS AND ELIMINATED THE NEED FOR THAT PARTICULAR SERVICE. THIS NINETEENTH-CENTURY ICE MAN SEEMS LIKE A CHARACTER OUT OF A COMEDY, BUT IN FACT HE WAS TYPICAL OF THE TIME.

beings had to find out what this strange "effluvia" was—or indeed had to become aware that it existed. Second, they had to figure out what they could do with it, if anything. There was a third story, too, for unraveling the secret of electricity played a large part in the creation of the scientific method, the way of thinking about the nature of things that in a few centuries has wrought the most amazing changes to life that humans have ever seen.

For several thousand years, people have been aware of two similar phenomena that fascinated and mystified them. At least as far back as 600 B.C.E., and probably well before that, people observed that if they rubbed the substance that we today call amber, light objects like straw and bits of hair would stick to it. This curious property of amber was first recorded by a Greek philosopher named Thales, although undoubtedly others before him had noticed the effect. Amber is resin exuded from pine trees which over a long period became fossilized and hard. Often lumps of amber can be found entangled in seaweed along the coast, where it has been washed up in storms. Small, soft lumps of resin recently secreted can be found on pine trees today. The Greeks called amber electron.

Another substance with puzzling properties similar to amber's was a certain type of dark ore able to draw pieces of iron to it. Chunks of this mineral were called lodestones (sometimes spelled *loadstone*). Early on, curious humans noticed that if a piece of the stone was allowed to move freely, for example, by floating on a board in a pan of water, the stone would line up in a north-south direction.

This material, an ore of iron, was apparently found in good supply in the ancient area of Magnesia—thus its name magnetite, or magnet. In time, people discovered that if a needle was placed near a lodestone, the needle would become magnetized as well and could be used to point the way north. This led to the invention of the compass, which the Chinese may have worked out more than three thousand years ago, although it is not certain. Through the centuries, the compass proved crucial in enabling early European mariners to make

PLUTARCH, ONE OF THE NOTED GREEK PHILOSOPHERS OF THE CLASSIC PERIOD, BELIEVED THAT MAGNETISM WAS CAUSED BY "STRONG EXHALATIONS" FROM THE LODESTONE.

the long sea voyages that helped to chart portions of the globe about eight hundred years ago. Without a compass, Columbus would not have been able to cross the Atlantic to find a world new to Europeans.

Yet, as curious as people were about these strange substances—lodestone and amber—for several thousand years they were not able to figure out how or why they worked. Plutarch, another ancient Greek philosopher, speculated that the lodestone "emits strong exhalations, which pushes the adjoining air." He theorized that the movement of the air would somehow carry a piece of iron toward the lodestone. Plutarch also pointed out that the lodestone would only attract iron, while amber would attract many kinds of light material. If so, how were these phenomena related?

Today we are so used to thinking scientifically that it is hard for us to grasp why it took so long for anyone to attempt to understand the amber effect better. We have to realize that people in general did not see things exactly as we do. There was a tendency to believe that the world had to be accepted as it was—there was no need to change anything. Indeed, in some religions people believed to force change would be to go against God. As a result, it didn't really matter how you explained phenomena like the movement of the sun and the stars, the tides, lightning, or death, as you weren't trying to do anything about them, anyway.

By the sixteenth century, a new way of thinking was becoming more widespread. Francis Bacon, an English philosopher, is often considered the first to insist on research as the key to knowledge and was thus the father of the scientific method. Over previous centuries countless others had made scientific explorations, but it was during the late sixteenth and early seventeenth centuries that a number of "natural philosophers," whom today we could call scientists, were consciously trying to think scientifically about matters that had mystified humans throughout history.

One of these was Jerome Cardan, a celebrated mathematician of the time. In 1550 he tackled the twin phenomena of amber and the lodestone by examining them in a critical way. Among other things, he noted, as Plutarch had, that magnets attracted only iron, while rubbed amber attracted straw, hair, chaff (husks of grain), and other light matter. But amber needed to be rubbed to become attractive, while magnets did not. And the effect could be blocked by a piece of paper placed between the amber and the light matter, while magnets worked through other objects. But Cardan did little testing and experimentation.

It was William Gilbert, an Englishman, who was really the first to take a scientific approach to the study of amber and magnetism. Gilbert, indeed, insisted that he was one of the pioneers of this new way of thinking, and he usually tested his conclusions before accepting them.

WILLIAM GILBERT WAS ONE OF A GROUP OF GREAT EUROPEAN THINKERS WHO WERE FORMULATING THE SCIENTIFIC METHOD IN THE SIXTEENTH CENTURY. THEY BELIEVED THAT IT WAS NOT ENOUGH TO HAVE IDEAS ABOUT A PHENOMENON: THERE HAD TO BE SOLID EVIDENCE SUPPORTING THEIR THEORIES.

He was born in 1544 in Colchester, the son of a well-to-do official. He studied medicine at Cambridge University, settled in London, and eventually became a leading doctor and personal physician to the famous Elizabeth I.

The late sixteenth century was an exciting time to be conducting scientific research. During Gilbert's lifetime, or thereabouts, Galileo, Francis Bacon, Copernicus, Johannes Kepler, and Descartes—to name just a few—were attempting to bring reason, careful observation, and experiment to bear on

ISAAC NEWTON IS CONSIDERED ONE OF THE GREATEST OF ALL SCIENTISTS—SOME SAY HE IS, IN FACT, THE GREATEST. HE NOT ONLY WORKED OUT THE THEORY OF GRAVITY BUT STUDIED MANY OTHER PHENOMENA, ESPECIALLY LIGHT AND COLOR.

questions that had long gone unanswered. Gilbert was part of this trend. As one scientific historian has said, "the beginning of the modern science of electricity" stems from Gilbert's famous work, *De Magnete* (*On the Magnet*).

Gilbert tested different materials and discovered that many of them would draw small objects to them when rubbed. He began to use the term *electrics* for objects that would act as amber did. He also invented a device that he called the versorium, a needle on a pivot which would turn toward the rubbed material. The versorium was the first electrical instrument.

Gilbert also undertook various experiments to test ideas about the cause of the amber effect and was able to dismiss ideas about "strong exhalations" and the like. He discovered certain types of materials that could not be electrified, in this way showing that materials fell into two groups, electrics and nonelectrics—or conductors and insulators, as we would say now.

But one important idea eluded him—a concept that students have trouble with even today. A little more than a half century after Gilbert published *De Magnete* in 1600, Isaac Newton, whom many consider the greatest of all scientists, brought forth his theory of gravity. To put it simply, this theory stated that two bodies are attracted to each other in proportion to their masses and the distance between them. This holds true whether we are talking about the planets and the sun or an apple falling from a tree to the ground. This theory required the existence of a force working at a distance. That is to say there is no material—no fluid, no tiny particles—between the two bodies that transfers the attractive force from one body to the other. The force of gravity works by itself over a distance.

Many people today have trouble with this idea of a force working at a distance, and so did William Gilbert and his fellow experimenters. Gilbert assumed that there had to be some physical intermediary, an ef-

An early artist's vision of von Guericke's machine for producing what we would now call static electricity. This drawing is almost certainly incorrect in some aspects: in all probability the handles would have been cranks, easier to turn than as shown. But it gives some idea of how von Guericke's device looked.

fluvium attracting objects to magnets and rubbed amber. Others after him also found themselves prone to believe in such an effluvium.

Gilbert's famous book *De Magnete* was widely read by people interested in the new scientific method. One who read it was an Italian named Niccolo Cabeo. He set up some experiments of his own and quickly noted an effect that Gilbert had missed: when an object attracted by an "electric" like rubbed amber hits the electric, it immediately shoots away. It is repelled, in a word. Here was one more thing to puzzle over: not only did electrics attract, they also repelled.

Through the years, electrical science slowly developed step-by-step as one person after the next added a little bit of knowledge or corrected earlier opin-

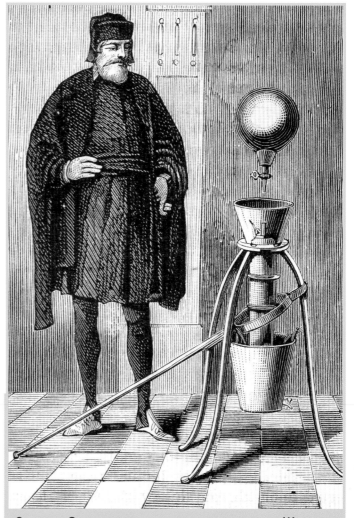

OTTO VON GUERICKE DEVELOPED A WORKABLE AIR PUMP. WITH THIS DEVICE, SCIENTISTS COULD CREATE GOOD VACUUMS FOR VARIOUS TYPES OF EXPERIMENTS.

ions. One of those who made the next steps was Otto von Guericke, mayor of Magdeburg in what is now Germany. Von Guericke invented the air pump and went on to develop an electrical machine as well. This was a ball or globe of sulfur, with a shaft running through the globe so that it could be turned by a crank handle. Sulfur, Gilbert had discovered, was one of those substances that acted like amber. As the handle was turned, a cloth or the hands could be held against the sulfur globe to produce the amber effect. Von Guericke's machine essentially provided a way of rubbing an "electric" at a high speed to produce a large quantity of what was still being called the effluvium.

But von Guericke was more interested in studying the earth's rotation than in electricity, and it was Francis Hauksbee, an Englishman, who is generally given credit for developing the electrical machine. Not much is known about him. He was probably a workman with a great mechanical ability. He was hired by the British Royal Society to build machines used to perform experiments. This group had recently been founded and was becoming the leading scientific body in the world. One machine Hauksbee built was similar to von Guericke's machine. Hauksbee used it for electrical experiments, though, and is therefore usually credited with being its inventor. With it, he discovered several important effects. For one, he found that if he held a glass tube close to an electrified globe, flashes of light would appear in the tube. This was yet another electrical mystery. For another, he found that if he hung threads from a frame around a spinning electrified globe, the threads would point straight toward the center of the globe rather than being blown around by the air currents normally produced by a spinning body. Hauksbee did not know what to make of this effect, either.

Hauksbee's work was published by the Royal Society, and eventually people interested in the new science became aware of his discoveries. One such person was Stephen Gray. As in the case of Hauksbee, we know little about Gray, except that he was living as one of the "poor brethren" at Charterhouse, a charitable organization that helped the poor, especially gentlemen who had fallen on hard times.

How Gray got interested in electricity we do not know, but in 1720 he sent a paper to the Royal Society on the subject. Nine years later, he began experiments to see if an electrified body could "communicate an electric-

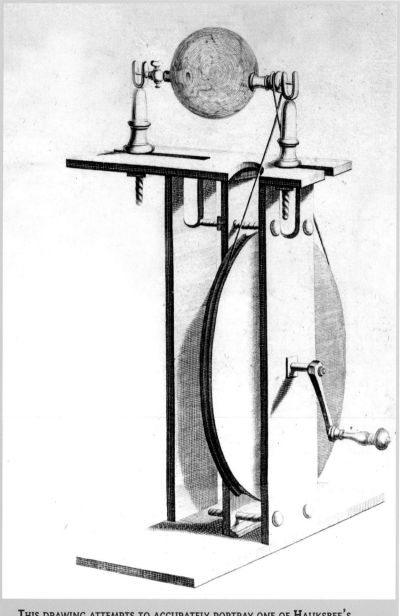

THIS DRAWING ATTEMPTS TO ACCURATELY PORTRAY ONE OF HAUKSBEE'S ELECTRICAL MACHINES. THE CRANK HANDLE SET IN MOTION A HEAVY WHEEL, WHICH NOT ONLY TURNED THE GLOBE ABOVE IT AT HIGH SPEED BUT ALSO WORKS AS A FLYWHEEL TO PROVIDE MOMENTUM. THE EXPERIMENTER WOULD HOLD HIS HANDS OR A CLOTH LOOSELY AROUND THE GLOBE, AND ELECTRICITY WOULD BUILD UP ON THE GLOBE'S SURFACE.

ity" to another body—the word *electricity* was now being used instead of *effluvium*. After putting corks in both ends of a hollow tube, he rubbed the tube to electrify it. A feather was attracted to the corks as well as to the glass itself, showing that the electricity had "communicated" to the corks.

The next obvious question was how far electricity would "communicate," or travel. He stuck a piece of fishing rod into the glass tube, put a cork on the other end of the rod and soon found that the attraction was carried the length of the rod. Gray wanted to extend the distance of the experiment, but his room in Charterhouse was too small. So he went to visit a friend in the country, a gentleman named John Godfrey, who had a large mansion called Norton Court. He and Godfrey quickly discovered that the electrical effect would travel along poles 28 feet (8.6 meters) long. They next tied a piece of packthread, or twine, to an 18-foot (5.5-meter) pole, for a total length of 52 feet (15.9 meters). The effect still worked.

Electricity, clearly, could be made to travel along various types of materials for considerable distances. In further experiments, Gray strung packthread from one end of a long room and back again, then in a large barn, and finally out of doors along poles for a distance of 650 feet (198.1 meters). Electricity traveled all these distances.

Gray had discovered one of the basic properties of electricity: conduction. The "effluvium," or more accurately current, could conduct itself long distances along certain types of materials.

During the course of these experiments, Gray discovered another central quality of electricity. In one case he had looped his packthread over a nail driven into a beam to keep it from sagging to the ground. This time the electrical effect had not worked. Gray correctly concluded that the electricity, instead of traveling the length of the string, had been drawn off by the nail.

In order to avoid this, he and his friend had decided that electricity was less likely to be drawn off if the packthread was hung from something very thin, rather than a thick nail. So they suspended the packthread from thin silk threads. The experiment worked, but the silk was not strong enough to hold the packthread up and subsequently broke. To prevent this, Gray substituted thin brass wire for the silk threads. Once again the experiment failed. Gray again concluded correctly that it was not the thickness of the supporting thread that mattered, but the material it was made of. Through his various trials, he had discovered an important truth: some materials—especially metals—are conductors, and some are nonconductors.

Gray's work was also published by the Royal Society. The group was now held in high esteem, and its papers were eagerly read by people interested in science. Similar societies would be started in other countries, but for a long time the Royal Society remained the major force in the field.

In France a well-to-do amateur scientist named Charles Dufay was following the Royal Society's reports. Dufay had been trained as a soldier but fell into bad health and retired to dedicate his life to science. In 1733 Dufay read about Gray's experiments. He then sent the Royal Society the results of his own work. He had discovered, he said, that virtually any material except metal and those too soft to be rubbed could be electrified. He had found that a line of packthread conducted electricity better if it was wet, and he had sent electricity a distance of 1,256 feet (383 meters).

His most important work, however, involved repulsion. As others had noted, a light body, like a feather or a piece of gold leaf, is normally attracted to an electrified glass tube. When it touches the tube, it is suddenly repelled. Allowed to touch another object, or fall to the ground, it will once again be attracted to the electrified tube. Dufay explained that when an unelectrified body touches an electrified one, it acquires electricity and is repelled. When it hits some other body, the electricity is drawn off; the object becomes unelectrified and can once again be attracted by an electrified body. Precisely how and why all of this happened Dufay did not know for sure.

He was even less sure when he took the experiment further. This time

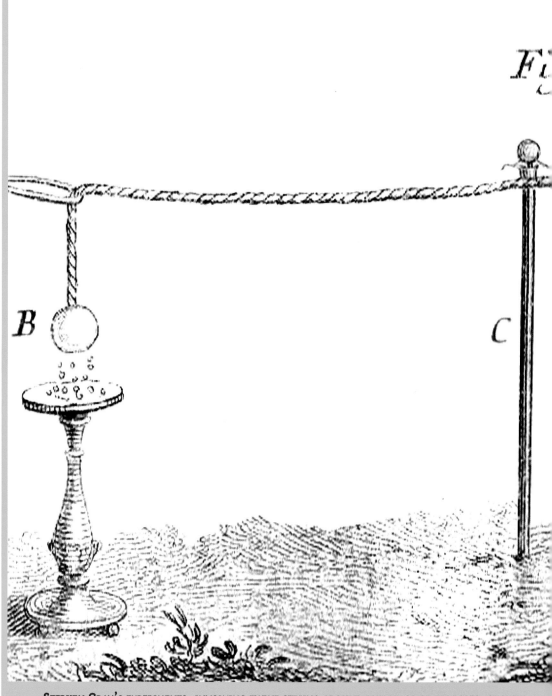

Fi

B

C

STEPHEN GRAY'S EXPERIMENTS, INVOLVING TWINE STRUNG AROUND BUILDINGS OR ON POLES, SHOWED THAT ELECTRICITY COULD BE CONDUCTED OVER LONG DISTANCES. THIS NOTION IS THE BASIS OF OUR ELECTRICAL SYSTEMS TODAY, IN WHICH POWER IS SOMETIMES CARRIED FOR HUNDREDS OF MILES FROM ITS SOURCE.

he electrified a piece of gold leaf by letting it touch a tube. The tube re-pelled the gold leaf, as expected. He then rubbed a chunk of copal (a hard tropical resin), electrifying it. He expected that it, too, would repel the gold leaf. Instead, it attracted it. The experiment, Dufay said, "disconcerted me prodigiously." He experimented further and in the end concluded that there were two types of electricity: "resinous" and "vitreous," or glasslike. Dufay was not correct in this conclusion, but he had stumbled on a hy-pothesis that other experimenters would shortly build on.

By this time, science had become of intense public interest. In-deed, it was something of a fad. Entertainers were putting on scien-tific demonstrations for pay in lecture halls and in the homes of the wealthy. One popular demonstration involved the recently invented air pump, which could empty a jar of air to create a partial vacuum. Demonstrators would put a twittering bird in a glass jar. As the air was sucked from the jar, the birdsong would gradually fade away, showing that sound needed the medium of air in which to travel. Demonstrations of electricity were even more startling, as experi-menters attracted bits of paper to glass rods and produced glowing light and crackling sounds. Growing out of these scientific spectacles was a popular belief that many phenomena that had for centuries seemed mysterious, and been attributed to magic, might have logical explanations.

However, the explanations—the "laws" of science—could only be discovered through the use of reason, the application of thought to provable facts. Speculation or guesswork would not provide answers. Only careful, well-thought-out experiments and study would solve the mysteries. There was an increasing belief that reason would reveal the solution to many human problems. Reason was the vehicle on which life would be improved. To many people of the time, the Age of Reason was arriving. Today we call this period—generally speaking the eigh-teenth century in Europe and America—the Enlightenment.

Looking back, we can see that a great many problems existing then were not solved by reason and have not been solved yet today, among them war, poverty, and many illnesses. But we can also see that the application of reason to the natural world—science, as we call it—did create miracles.

EARLY EXPERIMENTERS LEARNED TO PRODUCE SPARKS, FLASHES OF LIGHT, AND OTHER ELECTRICAL EFFECTS. BUT THEY WERE UNABLE TO FULLY GRASP EXACTLY WHAT IT WAS THEY WERE OBSERVING. NOT UNTIL NEARLY THE END OF THE NINETEENTH CENTURY DID SCIENTISTS UNDERSTAND THAT THESE PHENOMENA WERE CAUSED BY THE MOVEMENT OF ELECTRONS.

Lightning Rods and Batteries

In the century and a half between the experiments of William Gilbert and those of Charles Dufay, ingenious and curious people had pried open a door into the strange world of electricity. It was a world, they were discovering, where things did not always happen as they did in the world of common experience—where things ran according to comprehensible mechanical principles. Electrified bodies would attract or repel one another for no apparent reason. Electricity could be conducted for considerable distances along threads and wires. But what exactly was it?

Although Newton had made it clear that forces could work at a distance without any obvious physical connection, people still had trouble grasping the idea. In general, there was an assumption that electricity had to be a physical substance, possibly made up of particles so tiny that they could pass through solid bodies. Some believed that electricity was inherent in things, not a temporary condition, and could be "awakened" in a number of ways including rubbing. It would be some time before it was understood what electricity actually was. In fact, the nature of electricity was still not known when it was first being used to light homes and power machinery.

But interest in it remained intense, and through the eighteenth century experimenters added bit by bit to the understanding of it. A major

SOME EIGHTEENTH-CENTURY LEYDEN JARS. A CHARGE ON THE KNOB WAS CONDUCTED INTO THE JAR, WHERE IT WAS THEN STORED.

breakthrough came with the invention of the so-called Leyden jar. In 1745 E. G. von Kleist of Pomerania, in what is now Germany, inserted a nail into a bottle filled with water, so that the end of the nail stuck out of the bottle's neck. Using an electrical machine, like the ones devised by Hauksbee and von Guericke, he charged the nail. He then brought the nail close to an unelectrified body. An intense spark jumped across the gap. Von Kleist was of course holding the bottle in one hand. He then touched the nail with his other hand. He got a jolt that "stunned my arms and shoulders." He soon discovered that the device would remain charged for hours.

At around the same time, Pieter van Musschenbroek, a professor at the famous university in Leiden, Holland, also assembled a similar device. In his report on it he said, "I am going to tell you about a new but terrible experiment which I advise you not to try for yourself." In the course of working with the device, "Suddenly my right hand was struck so violently that all my body was affected as if it had been struck by lightning. . . . The arm and all the body are affected in a terrible way that I cannot describe: in a word, I thought that it was all up with me. . . ."

Scientific experiments became extremely popular in the eighteenth century, when it was believed that science—the rational study of the physical world—could vastly improve human life. It was mainly the wealthy who had time to witness such experiments. Here, Pieter van Musschenbroek demonstrates a Leyden jar, which is being charged by an electrical machine turned by a crank handle. The elegant lady is aiding in the experiment by using her hand to produce electricity on the spinning globe.

Although von Kleist had been slightly ahead of van Musschenbroek in working out the device, it became commonly known as the Leyden jar. In no time, other experimenters found ways to improve it, and it became extremely useful as a means of storing large quantities of electricity.

By then experimenters were routinely using wire to conduct electricity, which clearly traveled at a rapid rate. People had long noticed that sound traveled relatively slowly, as anyone could see by observing a man chopping wood from, say, a quarter of a mile: the ax would already be rising when the thunk was heard. Light, on the other hand, appeared to be instantaneous: it was visible immediately.

How fast, then, did electricity travel? Was it, like light, instantaneous, or did it travel at a measurable speed? Various experimenters tried to find out. The most conclusive evidence came in 1747 when a group of Englishmen sent a charge from a Leyden jar through a wire circuit 12,276 feet (3.7 kilometers) long—more than 2 miles (3.2 kilometers). The experimenters concluded that, like light, electricity moved from place to place instantaneously.

Americans, concerned with developing their new colonies, had devoted little time to scientific research. Only the wealthy had time to devote to experimentation, and most affluent Americans were occupied by their businesses. But anything that was fashionable in the Old World was of interest in the New World, and Americans had started going to scientific demonstrations brought over from Europe.

By chance, Benjamin Franklin happened to be in Boston when a demonstration of electricity was given. Franklin was a curious man, always eager to know how things worked, and he grew interested in the new science.

Benjamin Franklin is one of the great heroes of early America, and justly so. He rose up from a poor family to make himself wealthy as a printer, publisher, and writer. His essays and humorous writings are still fun to read today. He went on to play a major role in the creation of

America through his cleverness as a diplomat in England and France during the founding of the nation. In his lifetime, however, he was best known internationally for his experiments with electricity, especially the famous one with the kite and the key. Ben Franklin showed Europeans that Americans were not just rough farmers, but could be cultivated people of talent, indeed genius.

After seeing the demonstration in Boston, Franklin got hold of books and papers and read up on the subject. A friend sent him from England a glass tube of the kind being used to produce an electrical charge. Franklin had copies of it made for friends, and together they spent much time performing electrical experiments. He wrote a friend, "I never was before engaged in any study that so totally engrossed my attention and my time. . . ."

Because Franklin looms so large in the eyes of Americans, many tend to think of him as the discoverer of electricity. As should be clear, almost all the important work on electricity was done by Europeans. Nonetheless, Franklin made important contributions.

In one experiment he had two people stand on nonconducting, or insulated, platforms. One of them rubbed a glass tube with a piece of cloth. That man took the electricity from the cloth, while the other man took the electricity from the glass. When the two men brought their fingers close to each other, a strong spark passed between them. Afterward, the charge on both men was gone.

Franklin concluded that these two people had received electrical charges that were somehow opposite to each other. He performed other experiments to make the same point, finally announcing that Dufay had been wrong. There were not two types of electricity—vitreous and resinous, as Dufay had claimed—but only one type. All bodies seemed to naturally have the electric "fluid" in them. Rubbing one body displaced some of the fluid to the other, so that one had an excess of it, the other a deficiency. When the two men with opposite charges on them were brought together, electricity jumped from the body with an excess

LIGHTNING HAS ALWAYS CLAIMED HUMAN LIVES. BY THE EIGHTEENTH CENTURY, PEOPLE
CONDUCTING EXPERIMENTS IN ELECTRICITY WERE BEING SEVERELY SHOCKED OR EVEN KILLED
WHILE WORKING. HERE, AN EXPERIMENTER HAS BEEN KNOCKED DOWN DURING AN EXPERI-
MENT WITH LIGHTNING.

of it to the one with a deficiency. Franklin was the first to hit upon the idea of positive and negative charges, an important concept basic to the study of electricity. Unfortunately, in assigning positive and negative, Franklin got it backward: the electron flow is from what we call the negative to the positive. Still, Franklin's general concept was accurate and soon became widely accepted.

While the demonstration of positive and negative charges was undoubtedly Franklin's most important contribution to the growing body of electrical knowledge, his invention of the lightning rod was then, and is now, his most famous. Franklin was not the first to suspect that lightning and electricity were the same, or at least had properties in common, but he was the first to prove it. Moreover, he went on to show how lightning could be tamed.

For centuries lightning had been a terrible scourge. Every year hundreds of people were killed by lightning in Europe alone. Barns, often the tallest objects in the middle of empty fields, frequently caught fire after a lightning strike, resulting in the loss of human beings, livestock, and stores of food. Churches in particular were subjected to lightning bolts because, at the time, steeples were the highest points in most towns and cities. Making matters worse, it was believed that the ringing of the church bell high in the steeple would act as a plea to God to spare the church from lightning. During thunderstorms, hapless bell ringers were forced to pull the bell ropes. Many were electrocuted at their posts. Obviously, taming lightning would be a great blessing to humankind.

Franklin had observed that if you placed the blunt end of a rod close to a charged body, a spark would jump across the gap with a loud snap. However, if you offered a pointed rod instead, the electricity would be drawn off silently, bit by bit. If lightning was indeed just a form of electricity, could it not be absorbed slowly in the course of a storm, thus preventing it from striking anything or anybody? Franklin wrote a paper proposing an experiment in which a human being, sheltered in a

An artist's rendering of Benjamin Franklin's famous key-and-kite experiment. Actually, a Frenchman had been the first to test the effect, based on Franklin's ideas.

Safety First

The experiments run by early electrical scientists like Gray and Dufay were done with machines that generally produced relatively small amounts of electricity. They SHOULD NOT be tried with house current. The electricity that comes out of our wall sockets, or from the sockets in lamps we screw lightbulbs into, can kill and electrocute many people in the United States. You will not necessarily receive a fatal shock by touching a bare wire, but you easily can. You should never cut or scrape any kind of electrical wire unless you are sure it is unplugged. If you must remove a damaged lightbulb from its socket, make sure to unplug the lamp first. If the bulb is in a ceiling fixture that cannot be unplugged, shut off the power at the fuse box or circuit breaker. Just turning off the light switch will not necessarily cut off the electricity to the socket: it depends on how the fixture is wired, which cannot be known without testing it.

It is particularly dangerous to use an electrical appliance when taking a shower or bath. Every year Americans are killed when they accidentally drop a hair dryer or other appliances plugged into house current into the bath with them.

hut during a thunderstorm, would draw electricity through a rod or wire exposed to the air. He did not try the experiment himself, but some people in France saw his writings about it and performed it. The experiment worked: lightning was electricity and could be safely drawn off with the use of pointed rods or wires. Only later did Franklin himself try the famous experiment with the kite and the key.

Franklin then set about devising a practical lightning rod. This, too, worked. The invention made him a star in both America and Europe. Poems were written about him, portraits painted, medals bearing his profile sold as souvenirs. The effects of this fame had great importance. During the American Revolution, Franklin was sent to France to try to get support for the Americans from the French government. His great fame made it possible for him to meet anybody of importance he wished to see, and his reputation for genius made people listen carefully to what he had to say. French support of the new American government was vital to its victory over the mighty British army.

The experiments of Gray, Dufay, Franklin, and others continued to slowly unlock the secrets of electricity. But there was still a crucial element missing from the new science—measurement.

Today we know that we cannot fully understand a scientific phenomenon—light, heat, gravity, or whatever—until we can measure it. We need to know how big, how distant, how powerful a thing is in order to compare it with similar things. Nor can we usually make practical use of a phenomenon such as electricity until we can quantify it—that is to say, measure it.

Newton understood this. He not only came up with the idea of gravitational forces, he worked out a formula for determining their strengths. The force of gravity can be found by multiplying the masses of the bodies involved and dividing the result by the square of the distance. This has become known as the "inverse square law," simply as a matter of shorthand.

However, to make practical use of this or any formula, units of measurement—inches, pounds, acres, cubic centimeters—are necessary. Once the formula has been established, it doesn't matter what set of units is used, as long as it is consistently applied.

In Franklin's time, students of electricity had not yet come up with any formulas for the phenomena they were observing, much less units of measurement. But some were beginning to wonder if Newton's inverse square law would work for electrical forces as well as for the force of gravity. Several experimenters began working on ways to measure some of the factors involved. One such system worked like this, to simplify a good deal. A hollow metal bulb was floated in a bowl of water. This bulb was attached to a metal plate by a rod sticking out of the water. A second plate was positioned slightly above the first one. When the second plate was charged with electricity, it pulled the first plate toward it. This in turn raised the hollow bulb in the water. Small weights were then attached to the bulb. The amount of weight it took to pull the bulb back down to its original level could be used to measure the amount of charge on the plate. Using this and similar systems to compare various amounts of charge, experimenters concluded that the inverse square law did indeed apply to electrical force.

But these were very rough measurements. Something more accurate was needed. The man who came up with the answer was Charles Coulomb, a Frenchman. He had been studying various qualities of metals and had worked out a torsion balance, which could measure the force needed to twist various sorts of wires or rods. He was eventually able to measure forces as small as a 100-millionth part of a pound, which is a very small force indeed. But electrical forces can be quite small, and a highly sensitive instrument that was able to measure them was needed for good results.

Coulomb's mechanism of 1785 basically provided a way of measuring how much a given electrical force would twist a wire of known strength. The instrument had a circle marked off in the usual 360 degrees, as in a compass. The amount of twist could be read in degrees. With such a device, for example, Coulomb could record how much of the charge on an electrified body was lost by an action on it. He could also judge when bodies were equally charged, which was important to know for various experiments. Experimenters now had a valuable tool for the study of electricity.

Many of these experiments, like the ones Franklin had performed, involved human beings. This suggested that there might be some sort of "animal electricity" inside of living things. It was an exciting idea; perhaps electricity had something to do with the living spirit. At the very least, electricity might be the force that ran the human body.

As is the case today, there were ethical limits to the kinds of experi-

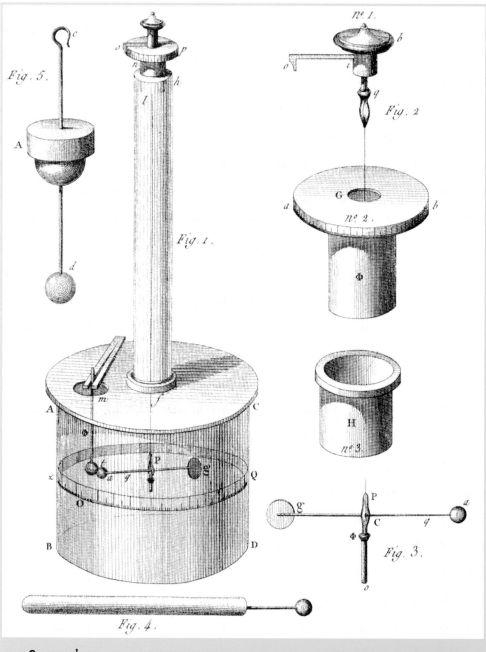

COULOMB'S TORSION INSTRUMENT, USED FOR MEASURING THE STRENGTH OF AN ELECTRICAL CHARGE, WAS, FOR THE TIME, A COMPLEX AND DELICATE DEVICE. THE STRENGTH OF THE CHARGE WAS INDICATED BY HOW FAR THE ARM INSIDE THE CONTAINER TURNED.

ments that could be run on humans, but tests could always be performed on animals. One scientist who believed in animal electricity was Luigi Galvani, a professor of anatomy at the University of Bologna. Galvani was interested in chemistry and physics as well as biology. One day in 1780 he happened to be dissecting a frog on a table where someone was using an electrical machine for some purpose. Apparently it was Galvani's wife who noticed that if the machine gave off a spark while Galvani was holding a scalpel at a nerve center, the frog's legs jumped. (We know today that the machine must have been inducing a current in the metal scalpel, which then entered the frog's nervous system.)

Intrigued, Galvani ran a series of experiments and found that he could get the legs to jump in many ways. While doing these experiments, he had some dead frogs hung up on brass hooks that passed through the animals' spinal cords. The hooks were hanging on an iron railing. Occasionally, by chance, a frog's legs would touch the iron railing as well as the brass hook it was hanging from. When this happened, the frog's legs would jerk. Galvani was convinced that he was on the trail of the famous animal electricity, but he was a careful scientist and did not publish his findings until 1791.

A professor at the University of Pavia named Alessandro Volta read about Galvani's frogs. He seriously doubted the idea of animal electricity. He concluded that the key to the effect was that different metals were touching a frog at the same time. Somehow the brass and iron together created a flow of electricity in the animal, which in turn made the legs jump.

Galvani and Volta got into an intense debate, each drawing followers to his side. In fact, both were partly right: animal electricity, in the way it was then understood, did not exist; but it is certainly true that small currents of electricity perform various tasks in the human system.

However, Volta's ideas about metals proved to be of enormous importance. After experimenting, Volta built an instrument in which disks

A sketch showing Luigi Galvani, with his back turned, experimenting with frogs. The woman beside him is presumably Galvani's wife, who is supposedly the person who first noticed that the frogs' legs twitched when there was an electrical spark nearby.

of zinc and copper were stacked up, with layers of felt, paper, or leather soaked in acid or brine between each pair. That is, there would be a disk of zinc, one of copper, and then one of an acid-soaked dividing layer. As Volta had hoped, when he attached wires to the bottom and top of the stack of disks, and brought the ends of the wires close together, a spark jumped across the gap. The stack, or voltaic pile, as it came to be called, was producing an electrical current.

The current was feeble compared to that produced by an electrical machine and stored in a Leyden jar, but the voltaic pile went on producing a current over an extended period of time, which the electrical machine didn't. With this machine Volta believed he had proved that the electricity that made Galvani's frogs' legs jump was produced by the contact of dissimilar metals. More important for the history of electricity, Volta had produced the first electric battery.

He probably created this voltaic pile in 1792, but he didn't

ALESSANDRO VOLTA DISPUTED THE IDEA THAT HUMANS WERE DRIVEN BY "ANIMAL ELECTRICITY." HE WENT ON TO PRODUCE THE FIRST STORAGE BATTERY, HIS FAMOUS VOLTAIC PILE.

publish a paper about it until 1800. So it was a tidy two hundred years between the publication of William Gilbert's *De Magnete*, which opened the investigation of electricity, and the voltaic pile, which would within one lifetime lead to a revolution in science. Millions of people born in the year that Volta published his work on the voltaic pile lived to see electricity lighting city streets.

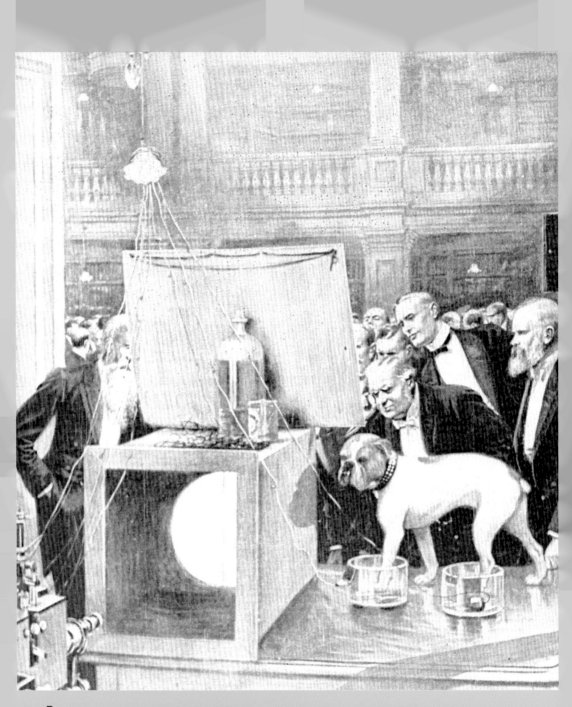

By the nineteenth century, public demonstrations of various scientific phenomena were common. Here, a dog is wired to a galvanometer in such a way that its heartbeats vibrate a wire which in turn moves the sheet dangling above. Often to the amazement of well-dressed observers, such demonstrations were as much entertainment as pure experiment.

The First Fruits

The speed with which the next developments in electricity took place is amazing. Within forty years after the introduction of the voltaic pile, scientists had discovered most of the basic principles of electricity—even if they still did not know exactly what electricity was.

The voltaic pile provided the key. The fact that electricity could be produced by the interaction of metals and an acid or salt solution suggested to researchers that chemistry was involved. Chemistry itself was a new science, but it was already further along than the science of electricity. In the second half of the eighteenth century, scientists had begun discovering and producing what we today know as the elements.

Among these pioneers was a young Englishman named Humphrey Davy. Born in 1778 into a moderately well-off family, Davy was able to get some education. He learned to read at five, at a time when the majority of people could not read at all, and as a youth wrote a lot of poetry. According to one of his friends, Davy "has a great deal of vivacity, talks rapidly and is so much interested in conversation that his excitement amounts to nervous impatience and keeps him in constant motion."

While barely out of his teens, Davy came to the attention of a strange man known as Count Rumford. He was an American, whose real name was Benjamin Thompson. He had made a good deal of money

THE FABULOUS AMERICAN BENJAMIN THOMPSON, BETTER KNOWN AS COUNT RUMFORD, SHOWN HERE IN A PORTRAIT BY THE ENGLISH PAINTER THOMAS GAINSBOROUGH. RUMFORD FOUNDED THE ROYAL INSTITUTION, WHERE BOTH HUMPHREY DAVY AND MICHAEL FARADAY MADE IMPORTANT STUDIES OF ELECTRICITY.

in America, but had sided with the British during the Revolution and had eventually fled to Europe. He reached Bavaria, where he had talked himself into a job as minister of war and was made a count. He made more money, moved to England, and became the moving spirit behind the Royal Institution, founded in 1799. The institution was supposed to investigate problems of the poor, but it quickly became a scientific institution.

Humphrey Davy, only twenty-two years old, became the head of it. He had been interested in various branches of science, but when the voltaic pile was invented, he decided to concentrate on electricity. He soon showed that the pile would not work when using plain water: an acid or saline solution was needed to produce electricity, which strongly supported the idea that a chemical reaction was involved. Other people began improving Volta's battery, and soon Davy had built a huge battery with which he was able to melt metals by passing a current through them. He noted, as others had, that these metals gave off considerable light when heated in such a manner.

With this great battery, Davy was able to produce another type of electrical light. When he ran a current across a gap, he got a continuous "sparking" effect—that is, an arc of electricity which produced a brilliant light. Here was the basis for electric-lighting systems developed a half century later.

The most important thing that Davy did, however, was to encourage a young man who would go on to become, according to one historian of science, "the greatest physicist of the nineteenth century and the greatest of all experimental investigators of physical nature."

Michael Faraday was born in 1791. His family was poor, and he was able to go to school only until he was thirteen, when he had to go to work. Fortunately, he got a job as an assistant to a bookseller and newsagent named George Riebau, who taught him how to bind books. Surrounded by books, the teenage Faraday became an assiduous reader. Once he was asked to bind an encyclopedia in which he hap-

THE GREAT SCIENTIST MICHAEL FARADAY. THE CIGAR-SHAPED OBJECT IN HIS HAND IS A BAR MAGNET, SIMILAR TO THE ONES FARADAY USED TO DEMONSTRATE THE PRINCIPLES THAT WERE BASIC TO ELECTRIC GENERATORS AND MOTORS.

pened on an article about the mysteries of electricity. He became entranced. Some of Riebau's customers developed an interest in this poor apprentice who seemed to have an intense curiosity about science. One of them gave Faraday tickets to hear one of Humphrey Davy's lectures at the Royal Institution. Faraday was swept up. He made careful notes on the lecture, which he illustrated with clever drawings, and sent them to Davy. He also built his own voltaic pile and began conducting his own experiments. Davy wrote young Faraday a kind response, but tried to discourage him from taking up a career in science—it was a hard way to make a living.

But Faraday would not be discouraged. As it happened, not long after sending the letter, Davy had to fire his assistant. He offered the job to Faraday, who jumped at the chance. Davy shortly married and set off on a honeymoon tour of Europe with his new wife, taking the twenty-one-year-old Faraday with them to help with various electrical studies he was conducting. (Davy's wife treated Faraday like a servant during the trip, which intensely annoyed the budding scientist.) For Faraday, the trip was a wonderful experience, because it allowed him to meet some of the greatest scientists in Europe, among them André-Marie Ampère, whom we honor every time we speak of amps.

Meanwhile, a brilliant professor at the University of Copenhagen in Denmark named Hans Christian Oersted made a critically important discovery. As early as 1812 Oersted had come to believe that magnetism and electricity were related. This was hardly a new idea: the Greek philosopher Plutarch had pondered the same question almost two millennia earlier. More recently, people had noticed that sometimes a piece of steel struck by lightning became magnetized.

In 1819 Oersted was performing an experiment for his students, using a voltaic pile. He noticed that the needle of a compass that happened to be lying nearby on the lab table jumped every time he turned the voltaic pile on and off. Oersted was struck by the effect, which certainly seemed to suggest some relationship between electricity and magnetism. Over the next few months he performed a number of experiments with magnets and electric currents. He discovered that not only could a current make a magnetized needle move, but that the process worked backward, as well: a wire carrying a current would move when in the presence of a magnet.

Oersted had discovered the basic principle of the electric generator and the electric motor, although he did not yet know it. He published this momentous finding in July 1820. Scientists were agog. Meanwhile, Ampère made another important discovery: two wires carrying parallel electric currents were drawn to each other, as if magnetized. In the fall of 1820 Ampère gave a series of lectures on this effect. At virtually the same time, François Arago found that a wire carrying a current would attract iron filings. Both he and Ampère also discovered that a wire wrapped around an iron bar would temporarily magnetize the bar when a current was run through the wire. Clearly, magnetism and electricity were related in some way.

These discoveries, coming along together, triggered a great deal of excitement among students of electricity. Michael Faraday was quick to seize on them. In September 1831, Faraday set a bar magnet upright in a cup of mercury. He then hung a wire down into the mercury near the magnet. When a current was sent through the wire, it began to rotate around the bar magnet.

Faraday then reversed the experiment. This time, instead of using a bar magnet, he positioned a magnetized steel needle, weighted at one end, so that it stood upright in the cup of mercury. The wire was fixed so that it could not move. So this time the magnet could move but the wire carrying the current could not. When the current went through the wire, the magnetized needle began to revolve around the conductor.

These experiments by various people gave rise to the concept of the field. This is a very important idea, which would eventually help to explain how many types of forces work. Faraday was perhaps most re-

ANDRÉ-MARIE AMPÈRE, WHOSE NAME GAVE US THE WORD *AMP*, DID IMPORTANT WORK IN UNRAVELING THE RELATIONSHIP BETWEEN ELECTRICITY AND MAGNETISM, A MYSTERY THAT HAD BEWILDERED THINKERS FOR AT LEAST TWO THOUSAND YEARS.

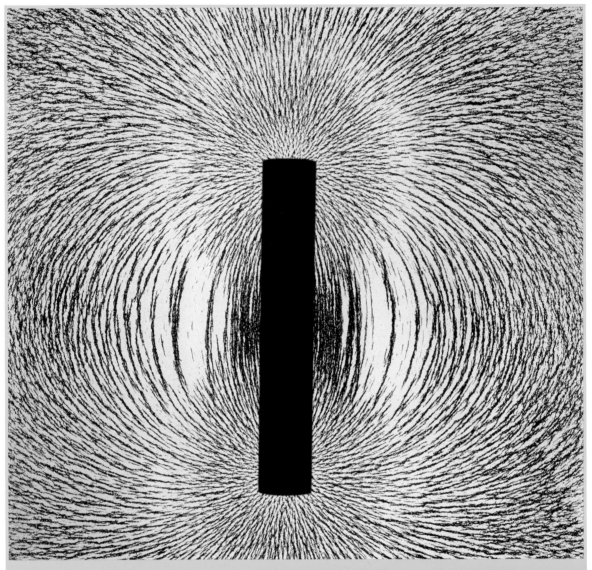

IRON FILINGS SCATTERED AROUND A MAGNET WILL QUICKLY FORM A PATTERN SHOWING THE LINES OF FORCE, IN THIS CASE CIRCLING FROM ONE END OF THE MAGNET TO THE OTHER. THIS EXPERIMENT CAN BE EASILY DONE AT HOME.

sponsible for the concept of the field, but others contributed as well. The idea applies to many areas of science. There are gravitational fields, magnetic fields, electric fields, and more. Today modern quantum mechanics has been able to satisfactorily explain the nature of fields. In Faraday's time, nobody knew exactly what a field was. However, Faraday and others saw that it was a useful idea. To simplify, a field is an area in which a force exerts itself. In some cases it is possible to actually see a field, which turned out to contain lines of force. Scatter iron filings around a magnet and they will form regular patterns showing the lines of force between the positive and negative poles of the magnet.

Given this concept, and the results of his experiments, Faraday concluded that if a current could make a wire move through a magnetic field, why wouldn't a wire

Amps, Watts, and Kilowatts

House current in the United States is run on 120 volts, although certain appliances, principally heating units, require 220. The amount of current that appliances use varies depending on the type of appliance. Heating units generally use a lot more electricity than lights or the small motors in fans and tape players. In most cases electrical appliances are rated in wattage. Watts are calculated by multiplying volts times amps. So, a 100-watt lightbulb in a house with a 120-volt system draws about .83 of an amp of current. A toaster rated at 1,200 watts, draws 10 amps of current.

Our electric bills are usually figured in kilowatt hours—that is to say, watts times the hours used divided by 1,000 to make the numbers simpler. So, if you use an air conditioner rated at 1,000 watts for six hours on a hot day, you will have burned 6 kilowatt hours of power. The cost of electrical power varies from place to place: in the author's home in upstate New York, the charge is about 10.6 cents per kilowatt hour. The 6 kilowatt hours used to run the air conditioner in the above example would cost about 64 cents.

moving through a magnetic field induce a current in the wire? Busy with other projects, Faraday could not tackle the problem right away.

But others were at work. Coulomb's torsion balance was able to measure the force of, or charge on, a given electrified body. Now a new tool, the galvanometer, was devised. It could measure the current or amount of electricity flowing through a conductor, whether it was a

GEORG SIMON OHM STUDIED THE PHENOMENON OF RESISTANCE AND DISCOVERED THAT IT VARIED ACCORDING TO THE SIZE OF THE CONDUCTOR AND THE TYPE OF MATERIAL IT WAS MADE OF. HE WENT ON TO WORK OUT A FORMULA FOR CALCULATING RESISTANCE, WHICH TODAY IS MEASURED IN OHMS.

wire or the nervous system of a frog. Think of water being driven through a hose: the charge is like the water pressure; the current is like the amount of water running through the hose. Today we measure the charge in volts and the current in amperes, or amps. The total amount of electricity being used is found by multiplying the volts times the amps and is measured in watts.

There is a third ingredient, which was identified by an investigator named Georg Simon Ohm. In 1825 Ohm began studying the current flowing through various kinds of conductors. He soon discovered that the current varied greatly depending on the size of the conductor and the material it was made of. This was a fact that people had known in a general way for a long time, even back in the days when Hauksbee and Gray realized that some materials were better conductors than others.

Ohm, however, by making careful measurements, was able to work out the rule that bears his name today: the current through a conductor equals the force, or voltage, divided by what is termed the resistance. Metals like gold and copper have little resistance and conduct well; wood has higher resistance and conducts poorly. The resistance of a material is today measured in ohms.

With these new tools available, in 1831 Faraday finally set about trying to show that magnetism could be used to produce electricity. He found the key by thrusting a bar magnet rapidly into the center of a coil of wire attached to a galvanometer. When he did so, the needle on the galvanometer jumped, indicating a current in the coil of wire. When he withdrew the magnet, the needle jumped again although this time in the opposite direction. Faraday concluded that the change of the magnetic field induced a current in the wire. It was clear that the magnetic field could be changed in respect to the wire in either of two ways: move the wire or move the magnet.

Faraday went on to build a device in which a copper disk was spun through the arms of a horseshoe magnet. When the disk turned, a current was induced in it. This was the first true electric generator, but it was far too inefficient to be a practical source of electricity.

Somebody asked Faraday, "What is the use of it?"

He replied, "What is the use of a new-born baby?"

Meanwhile, in the United States, another electrical genius was following a course similar to the one Faraday's life had taken. Joseph Henry was born in 1797, six years after Faraday. Like Faraday, he was unable to get much education, and like Faraday, he became a passionate reader. At the age of sixteen, while at home because of an injury, he found a book on science. He became fascinated, as Faraday had been, while reading about electricity and grew determined to become a scientist. He managed to get some education and then got a job as a teacher at Albany Academy. There he began his serious experiments with electricity.

His first investigations involved electromagnets. He invented one that could lift 9 pounds (4.1 kilograms) and eventually went on to build even larger ones. In 1831, just as Faraday was working on electrical induction, Henry produced an electromagnet for Yale University that could lift more than a ton. He also discovered another phenomenon that would have major effects years later. He had seen that lightning striking several miles away could magnetize steel needles. To figure out how electricity might travel over a great distance, he strung a wire circuit around the top floor of a building and placed another similar circuit in the basement. He found that when he ran a current through the upper circuit, a needle attached to the lower circuit became magnetized. This was not, he decided, a simple case of electrical induction. Something else was occurring, and he suggested that it might be due to some kind of waves similar to light. Henry was getting close to the idea of the electromagnetic spectrum, a rainbow of waves vibrating at different speeds, and including radio waves, visible light, X-rays, and infrared rays. However, it was left to others to make the leap of imagination.

Henry was by now famous both in the United States and Europe, where he was seen as the first American since Franklin a hundred years earlier to contribute to the science of electricity. When the Smithsonian Institution in Washington, D.C., was founded in 1846, Joseph Henry was asked to become its first director.

By chance, some of the people who were making these great strides in the science of electricity had been mainly self-educated, among them Davy, Henry, and Faraday. While they were brilliant scientists, none had a particularly strong background in mathematics. As a consequence, they showed how certain things worked, but they missed some of the implications of what they suspected—as Henry had done in the matter of waves. However, a young man was coming along who would break through their limits.

James Clerk Maxwell, born in 1831, came from a long line of small Scottish landholders. His father earned a modest but steady income from his lands. Maxwell's mother died when James was only eight, and his father raised him alone. Deeply religious, the boy was known for his sense of humor and twinkling black eyes. In childhood he was always asking, "What's the go o' that?" meaning, "How does it work?" As a schoolboy, he devised a method of drawing ovals that was better than the one his teachers were using. It was clear that he was a very promising boy. When he had completed his initial schooling, his father sent him to famous Cambridge University. There Maxwell studied mathematics, and in 1873 he applied mathematics to several of the laws of electricity discovered earlier by Faraday and others. He was able to do what these pioneers had not done—work out formulas. Among his figurings were formulas for electric and magnetic fields, which showed how lines of force in these fields behaved.

He went still further. He saw that there were gaps in his equations; and in mathematically filling in the gaps, he came across the concept of waves, which Henry and others had speculated about. Maxwell then concluded that light was an electromagnetic wave. Not long afterwards Heinrich Hertz, a German, proved the existence of these waves, and soon various scientists identified the individual elements that make up the

James Clerk Maxwell applied the advanced math of his time to electrical phenomena and, in the end, was able to infer the existence of electromagnetic waves. Soon after, Heinrich Hertz proved the existence of these waves, which are the basis of radio, television, X-rays, and much else.

electromagnetic spectrum of waves. Within a generation, further study of waves would bear fruit in the development of radio, X-rays, and other devices. Like many phenomena of modern science, they could only be truly understood through mathematics. It had taken just a single human lifetime to move from the voltaic pile to the theories of fields and waves. The door was now open to harness electricity and use it for the benefit of all.

THROUGHOUT MOST OF THE WORLD'S HISTORY, PEOPLE HAD TO WORK BY DAYLIGHT OR NOT AT ALL. HERE, PEASANTS IN ABOUT 1600 HARVEST WHEAT IN NORTHERN EUROPE. ONCE DARKNESS FELL, THE DAY WAS OVER FOR THESE LABORERS.

Electricity Lights the World

For most of human history, people have operated by the sun, the moon, and the stars. People became active when the first light broke in the east an hour or so before sunrise and slept as twilight turned into night. Occasionally, people were active at night: even into the time of Faraday and Maxwell, farm families sometimes worked in the hay fields by moonlight to take advantage of good weather. But in general, work ceased at dark.

Of course among the rich, who could afford to burn a lot of candles, work and play might take place after dark. But even for them, dinner—the main meal of the day—was eaten during daylight hours. For most people, the evening meal was a quick supper that did not need a lot of preparation. By the mid-nineteenth century, this pattern was beginning to change in the industrial world as kerosene and various forms of inflammable gas were invented or discovered. It was then possible to extend the day past twilight. Even so, for many, if not most, families, oil and gas were costly, and early to bed and early to rise remained the rule. Our current way of life, which allows for a long evening of work or play, has been possible only for the last tiniest fraction of human history. And it has been due almost wholly to our taming of electricity.

Faraday had shown in 1831 that a current could be induced in a wire by moving the wire through a magnetic field. It was obvious to

An early dynamo for generating electricity. The horizontal tubes on the top and bottom were electromagnets. The central wheel is essentially composed of wires that are spun through the magnets' fields of force, inducing electrical currents in the wires.

many people that here was a system for generating electricity, if the mechanics of it could be ironed out.

The first person to come up with a workable solution was—probably—Hyppolite Pixii, a Frenchman who built a small machine, using permanent magnets, that could produce a current. He was followed by others. Soon researchers found that using an electromagnet rather than a permanent one was more efficient. In about 1869 a professor of physics in Brussels, Belgium, produced what came to be called a dynamo. It generated 50 volts of electrical charge. The machine was used primarily for electrochemical work, especially for breaking down water into oxygen and hydrogen, for which there were many uses. Quickly, the use of dynamos became more widespread, and soon it was clear that it would be possible to generate large amounts of electricity.

The idea of harnessing electricity to produce light had been around for some time. Experimenters had made glass tubes glow and had produced sparks and crackling like lightning in their demonstrations. Most significantly, Humphrey Davy had sent a continuous spark across a gap to create an arc of light.

With dynamos readily available, inventors looked for a way to make arc lamps. The first use of arc lighting—indeed, the first practical use of electricity for lighting of any kind—came in 1858 when Faraday supervised the installation of arc lighting in the South Foreland Lighthouse in England. Development of arc lighting thereafter was rapid. Many different systems were worked out, all depending on the continuous flow of electricity across a gap.

In most cases the points from which the electricity flowed were made of carbon, which could withstand high heat. Nonetheless, over time these carbon points burned away and had to be replaced. Improvements allowed them to last long enough to be practical. Arc lighting was too bright, and flickered too much, to be of use in homes and was in other ways not practical. It was mainly used for street lighting, although it was sometimes used in stores, theaters, dance halls, and other public spaces as well. By the mid-1880s arc lighting was being widely used in both the United States and Europe.

ALTHOUGH THOMAS ALVA EDISON IS ALMOST ALWAYS CREDITED WITH HAVING INVENTED THE LIGHTBULB, AN EARLIER VERSION WAS DEVELOPED IN ENGLAND BY SIR JOSEPH WILSON SWAN. HOWEVER, EDISON WAS AN IMPORTANT PIONEER WHO WENT ON TO BUILD THE FIRST SUCCESSFUL ELECTRICAL SYSTEM.

The next challenge was to bring electric light into homes. It had long been observed that if a strong current was passed through a piece of metal, it would become hot enough to glow and eventually melt. The trick would be to find a way to heat a material to incandescence, as it was termed, without burning it away. By the 1840s various experimenters were searching for practical ways to produce this incandescent effect. They found materials that would glow for short periods, but then would burn out, often producing smoke that blackened the surrounding glass. For nearly thirty years, from the 1840s into the 1870s, scores of inventors struggled with the problem of creating a workable incandescent lightbulb. One solution was to surround the filament with a vacuum, as nothing can burn without oxygen. At first the air pumps available were not efficient enough to create a sufficient vacuum. In 1865 an improved air pump solved that problem.

Finding a material that would burn very slowly proved more difficult. Finally, in 1878 an Englishman named Joseph Swan made a workable version of an electric lightbulb, using a carbon filament. Says one historian of electricity, "There is considerable justification for the claim that Swan rather than Edison was the inventor of the incandescent lamp. . . ."

Nonetheless, Thomas Alva Edison was the man who built the first practical electric-lighting system and who made home lighting feasible. Edison was born in Ohio in 1847. He was such a slow learner as a child that his teachers despaired of him. He was taken out of school and taught at home by his mother. From boyhood, he showed an ambition and a strong desire to advance himself. He sold newspapers and candy on trains and took an interest in the new system of telegraphy that was rapidly spreading across the nation. Telegraph operators needed to be able to translate the dots and dashes of Morse code into letters at high speed. Edison got a job as a telegraph operator and soon proved to be one of the fastest.

He had always had an interest in science and a talent for invention. This period, the second half of the nineteenth century, was the greatest age of innovation the world has ever seen. Radio, sound recording, the movies, the automobile, the airplane, high-quality steel, and advanced

THOMAS EDISON WAS ONE OF THE MOST FAMOUS MEN OF HIS TIME, GENERALLY BELIEVED TO BE A SCIENTIFIC GENIUS. IN FACT, HE WAS MORE OF A DEVELOPER OF IDEAS, SOME HIS OWN AND SOME PRODUCED BY OTHERS. HE WAS A DETERMINED MAN WHO KNEW HOW TO SELL HIS IDEAS TO INVESTORS AND THE PUBLIC.

manufacturing systems all came out of that time. Inventors were growing rich, and many young people were looking for new ways of doing
things that would make their fortunes. A young man working in a barn
without much money could come up with an idea worth millions. In
Germany, Benz and Daimler built the first true automobiles in their
own small shops; the Wright brothers built the first practical airplane in
their bicycle shop. Edison took his place in this great movement that
was creating the industrial world.

In 1868 he got a job with the Western Union Telegraph Company.
Soon afterward, he produced his first machine: an electromagnetic vote
recorder. He rapidly went on from there and within a few years had set
up his own company. In 1876 he built his famous invention factory in
Menlo Park, New Jersey. There, with a staff of assistants, Edison worked
on a variety of projects that made him both rich and famous.

In truth, Thomas Alva Edison was more important as an organizer
and businessman than as an inventor. He invented the first sound-
recording machine, but many of the other things he has been credited
with, like the movie projector, were actually improvements on earlier
models initially made by others.

This was certainly true of the incandescent lightbulb. Many others
had been working on the lightbulb before him. Some had come close,
and Joseph Swan had apparently produced a practical bulb. It was left
to Edison to develop a whole system of lighting.

In 1877 he began to work on the problem, testing hundreds of different materials in search of one that could be used for a filament. He tried
various metals, paper, wood, even bamboo and palm leaves. Finally, in
1879, he produced a lightbulb with a carbonized thread filament that
burned for forty-five hours before it went out.

Edison was thorough by nature and did not stop there. He went on
testing, and curiously enough, discovered that carbonized bamboo
made the best filaments. For several years, filaments in Edison lightbulbs were made of bamboo, until better materials were found.

Edison now had to capitalize on the invention. At this he was a mas-

A SCALE MODEL OF THE FIRST CENTRAL POWER STATION, THE FORERUNNER OF MANY THOUSANDS TO COME. EDISON'S GENIUS LAY IN CONNECTING AN ENTIRE ELECTRICAL SYSTEM, WHICH BEGAN THE WIRING OF THE WORLD.

ter. A great publicist, he was already vastly admired and had no trouble getting backing for his proposed electrical system. The first one was installed on the steamship *Columbia,* which was then being constructed.

The *Columbia* had its own power plant. Edison went on to install electrical systems in a great many factories with their own power plants. However, he realized that it would be far more economical to build a central power station from which wires would radiate through the surrounding area. The first Edison Central Station was built on Pearl Street, in New York City. It went into operation in September 1882. From there, buildings were wired and meters installed in an area of about one-sixth of a square mile.

The new power system proved to be an unqualified success. Immediately orders flooded in for similar systems—and not just from America, but from Europe and elsewhere as well. Other inventors devised their own types of lightbulbs, and the electrification of the world shot ahead.

It was, however, mainly cities that were being wired for electrical power. There were still serious problems with delivering electricity to the millions of

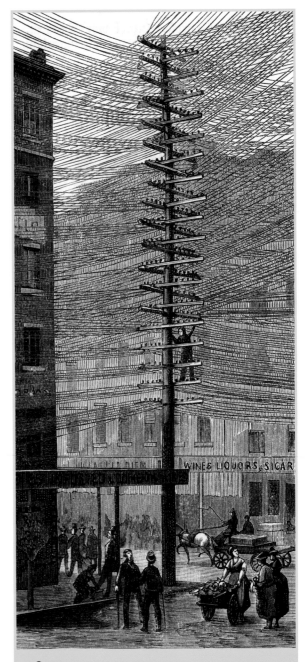

ONE RESULT OF THE ELECTRICITY BOOM WAS THE APPEARANCE OF A VAST SPIDERWEB OF ELECTRIC (AND TELEPHONE) LINES STRUNG THROUGH THE NATION'S LARGEST CITIES. TODAY MOST WIRES, IN CITIES AT LEAST, ARE LAID IN UNDERGROUND PIPES; BUT POWER LINES AND NETWORKS OF WIRES ARE STILL VISIBLE IN THE SUBURBS AND THE COUNTRYSIDE.

people living in the American countryside. For one thing, in a city a power line a few hundred feet long could connect to buildings occupied by hundreds of people. In the country several miles of power lines might be needed to connect to just three or four rural families. Delivering power to the countryside was far more expensive than channeling it through a city.

For another, an electrical current loses power as it travels. This is not a problem over short distances, but if a current is carried for more than a half mile or so, the loss of power is significant. The answer was to send the power out at high voltages and then step down the voltage as it entered local areas. However, this was not easy to do with direct current, the kind of electricity that had almost always been produced.

Direct current, or DC as we usually say, is the movement of electricity in one direction around a circuit, which begins at the power plant, flows through power lines into a house, passes through a lightbulb or electric motor, and returns via power lines to the source.

But electrical current did not have to travel around and around, like a merry-go-round. It could instead move rapidly back and forth: it was not the direction of the current that mattered, but the fact that it was in motion. For example, a board can be cut with a saw blade that runs continuously around and around in the same direction, like a circular saw; but it can be cut just as well with a blade that goes rapidly back and forth, as in a jigsaw or saber saw. So it is with electricity.

An electrical current, thus, can alternate. As it happened, alternating current, or AC, could be much more easily stepped up and down in voltage. Faraday, Henry, and others had produced transformers that would raise or lower the voltage of an electrical current. In this way, AC could be sent long distances by jacking up the voltage to several thousand volts and then bringing it back down to a much lower voltage before it went into the wires of a house.

AC did have its disadvantages. There were no motors, in 1882, that would work on alternating current; AC could be used for lighting, but not for running factory machines. Also, AC generators had certain problems that DC models did not.

NIKOLA TESLA DEVELOPED THE FIRST ELECTRIC MOTOR THAT WOULD WORK USING ALTERNATING CURRENT, MAKING TODAY'S ELECTRICAL SYSTEMS POSSIBLE. HE ALSO DID IMPORTANT WORK ON THE BASIC PRINCIPLES OF RADIO. HE IS SHOWN HERE IN HIS LABORATORY IN ABOUT 1910, WHEN HE WAS AT THE HEIGHT OF HIS FAME.

Once again, as always in the science of electricity, a number of people contributed to the solution of this problem. But the key figure was a strange genius named Nikola Tesla.

Born in 1856 in Croatia of Serbian parents, Tesla proved to be a child prodigy, who was skilled in math and had an incredible memory. As an adult he developed a great fear of germs, which caused him to wash his hands again and again each day. He avoided coffee and tea, but drank whiskey. He couldn't stand to touch hair and never married.

He studied at the well-known university in Graz, Austria, and then in Budapest. Walking in a park there in 1882, an idea for a complete system for an AC motor suddenly flashed through his mind. However, he was poor, without connections, and could find no way to get the backing needed to develop his vision.

He next went to Paris, where American technicians were installing the Edison lighting system. Some of the Americans he met recognized Tesla's abilities and suggested that he go to the United States. Once there, Edison, too, recognized his genius and hired him. Within a year Tesla decided, rightly or wrongly, that Edison had failed to pay him some promised money and Tesla left. He was then totally without money and for a while worked as a ditchdigger to support himself. But by 1886 Tesla had managed to develop his AC motor and had patented it.

Meanwhile, a wealthy businessman named George Westinghouse, who had invented air brakes for railroad trains and had built the company that is still well known today, was among other things manufacturing signaling equipment for railroads. So he was in the electrical business.

In 1885 Westinghouse heard of an AC system being used in Europe that ran on 2,000 volts, which were stepped down by transformers for home lighting. Westinghouse installed the system in a few small American cities.

In May 1885, Nikola Tesla read a paper to a meeting of the American Institute of Electrical Engineers on his AC motor. Westinghouse heard about it. He instantly seized on it as the answer to the shortcomings of

NIKOLA TESLA SEEN SEATED IN HIS LABORATORY, SURROUNDED BY ARTIFICIAL LIGHTING. PICTURES LIKE THIS ONE ADDED TO TESLA'S REPUTATION AS A WILD GENIUS.

LIKE SO MANY OTHER INVENTORS OF THE NINETEENTH CENTURY, GEORGE WESTINGHOUSE WAS BORN IN MODEST CIRCUMSTANCES. HE HAD HIS FIRST SUCCESS WITH THE INVENTION OF THE AIR BRAKE, WHICH DRAMATICALLY IMPROVED RAILROAD SAFETY. HE WENT ON TO BUILD THE HUGE COMPANY THAT BEARS HIS NAME. HE WAS RESPONSIBLE FOR FORCING ACCEPTANCE OF THE ALTERNATING-CURRENT SYSTEM, WHICH EVENTUALLY PUSHED ASIDE EDISON'S DIRECT-CURRENT SCHEME.

his AC systems. He bought Tesla's patents for $1 million, a huge amount of money for the time, and hired Tesla to help with the development of the AC system.

Thomas A. Edison had committed himself to the direct-current system, which he had developed. He was determined to fight Westinghouse's competing AC system. Edison told the press that AC was dangerous because of the high voltages involved. To prove it, he had a horse publicly electrocuted by AC power.

Westinghouse fought back. A huge world's fair was being planned for Chicago. The new, amazing electric lighting would be featured. Westinghouse saw to it that he got the contract for the lighting. The brilliant lights flooding the Chicago Exhibition, powered by alternating current, amazed visitors who were still lighting their homes with kerosene and gas lamps. The Chicago Exhibition gave the Westinghouse system the publicity and exposure it needed.

At the same time, plans were being hatched to use the tremendous weight of water flowing over Niagara Falls as a source of power. Many ideas were proposed, but by the late 1880s there was general agreement that the falls should be used to generate electric power. After much argument, it was decided to use Westinghouse's AC system. Work began in 1890, and by 1895 AC power was being delivered to factories using machines based on Tesla's ideas.

But Tesla, prickly and independent, had left Westinghouse. He had made a lot of money from his work with Westinghouse, and he began spending it on research into radio waves. Today we generally credit Guglielmo Marconi with "inventing" radio, but it is now clear that Tesla first discovered many of the principles involved.

Once again, however, Tesla did not follow up on his own ideas, but instead turned to new fields. He was determined to find a way to send power by radio waves, and while he was pursuing this fanciful notion, others made major advancements in radio and related fields like X-rays and radioactivity. Still, says one historian, Tesla, "established the essen-

THE WORLD'S COLUMBIA EXHIBITION OF 1893 IN CHICAGO WAS A HUGE SUCCESS AND DREW A VAST NUMBER OF INTERNATIONAL VISITORS. THE SPECTACULAR LIGHTING PROVIDED BY WESTINGHOUSE'S ALTERNATING-CURRENT SYSTEM GAVE AC A GREAT DEAL OF PUBLICITY.

tial elements of radio communication." One other important contribution made by Tesla was to work out the electrical standards in use today. Scientists had long wondered how fast the alternating cycles of AC ought to be. In some early AC systems the frequency was 25 cycles a second, in some as many as 130. Tesla decided that 60 cycles was the best compromise, and that is what we use in the United States today. House current is usually 120 volts, although 220 is often required for certain appliances, like electric stoves. In Europe 50 cycles is more common and house current is often 220 volts, which is why some American appliances, like CD players, will not work properly in Europe, unless run through an adaptor.

The great success of the Niagara Falls electrical system effectively ended direct-current systems. Although a few lingered on for decades, it would be an AC world. Quickly, cities and towns were electrified: by the 1920s gas lighting was going out of use in populated areas. It would be another twenty years before electrification would catch up to rural areas; not until after World War II was electrical service generally available everywhere in America. But it had been only seventy years since the moment Edison's Pearl Street power station had sprung into action, inaugurating the age of electricity—a very short time as history goes.

BEFORE ABOUT 1830 TRAVEL IN AMERICAN CITIES WAS UNDERTAKEN BY HORSE OR BY FOOT. HERE, PEOPLE WALK, AS A CARRIAGE DRIVES THROUGH NEW YORK CITY'S BOWLING GREEN, AN AREA HOME TO SKYSCRAPERS TODAY.

Traveling by Electricity

Transportation has always been a main human concern. It has particularly been so for Americans, who inhabit a large country. Even today Americans usually travel much farther to get to work, to shops, to places of entertainment, than people in most other places.

Before the middle of the nineteenth century, most Americans lived on farms and traveled, when they had to, on foot or by horse, mule, or ox cart. Long-distance travel was usually by water. However, by the 1840s railroads were being built, and railroad travel was becoming commonplace for journeys from town to town.

Before 1830 America's cities were small: New York had about 125,000 inhabitants, Boston 45,000, Cincinnati about 10,000. City dwellers could get to where they needed to go by foot or on horseback.

But beginning in the 1830s, America's cities began to grow rapidly, swelled by both immigrants coming from Europe and people leaving their farms. These new city dwellers mainly worked in the factories springing up, born of the new technologies. Cities spread out into the countryside, where fields and forests had once been. The new cities of the nineteenth century might cover several square miles, too large to be walked through in a reasonable amount of time.

At first the answer lay in horse-drawn coaches. By the 1830s coaches were running through city streets on rails, much like the ones carrying today's trains. Through the next several decades horse-drawn streetcars were installed in most American cities. By the 1860s some of these streetcars were running on elevated railways two stories above the streets. Elevated railway cars were pulled either by steam power or cables drawn from a central point.

But the horse-drawn vehicles were slow. There was a second problem: as cities grew, the number of horses using the streets multiplied. Horse manure and urine were a constant presence. Tons of waste had to be removed from city streets each day. Not only was it unpleasant, but it was a source of disease as well. So the search was on for machines to replace horses.

The idea of using electricity to drive machinery was an old one. In the eighteenth century, little "whirligigs," which spun around when electrified, had been developed, but they had no practical use. The first true electric motors were developed only after Joseph Henry and others had worked out powerful electromagnets. These motors employed walking beams, on the seesaw principle. An electromagnet pulled down one end of the walking beam. As soon as it reached the bottom of its rotation, a second electromagnet pulled down the other end of the beam. By running electrical power alternately through two electromagnets, the arm could be kept rocking back and forth to drive a piece of machinery. In the 1830s several inventors worked out walking-beam motors of this kind. The best was built by Thomas Davenport, a Vermont blacksmith, in 1834. It was powerful enough to operate a small electric railway.

But something better was needed, and it was discovered by chance, as is often the case. At an exposition in Vienna in 1873, there was a demonstration of an electric generator. While one of the generators was operating, a workman accidentally connected its wires to another generator, sending an electric current through it. This second generator began to spin. The person in charge instantly saw the significance of the

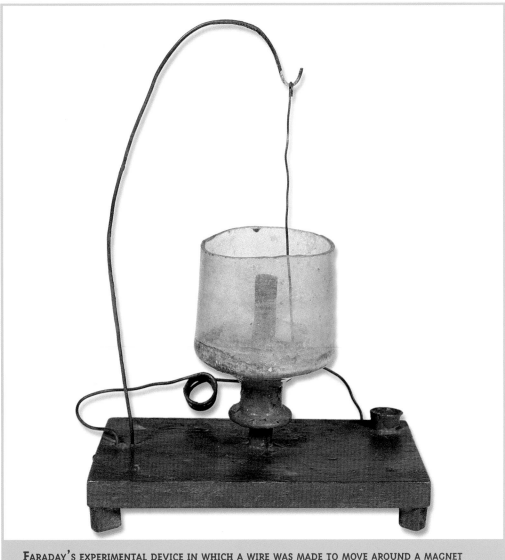

FARADAY'S EXPERIMENTAL DEVICE IN WHICH A WIRE WAS MADE TO MOVE AROUND A MAGNET WHEN A CURRENT WAS SENT THROUGH THE WIRE. WITH THIS EXPERIMENT, FARADAY DEMON-STRATED THE BASIC PRINCIPLES OF ELECTRIC GENERATORS AND MOTORS.

accident: an electric motor was simply the reverse of an electric generator. The generator, turned by steam or some other source of power, produced electricity; in a motor, electricity caused the machine to revolve.

Why this had taken so long to work out is hard to understand. Faraday and others had shown that if you ran a current through a wire, it would move around a magnet. But the principle was now clear, and soon electric motors much like the ones we use today were being produced.

Electric motors could be used to drive factory machines. They could also be used to propel carts and carriages. So, interest in self-propelled carriages was high: tinkerers were already trying to design horseless carriages driven by the new internal-combustion engine, which used gasoline. Electricity promised cleaner, quieter power.

The first to manage the feat was most likely Werner von Siemens, founder of the well-known Siemens company. In 1879

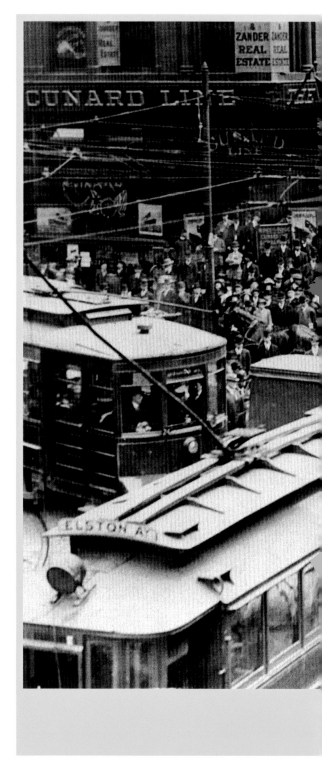

It did not take automobiles to create traffic jams, as this scene in Chicago in 1909 reveals. In the foreground is a classic trolley car, showing the trolley on the end of a pole that ran along the electrical wire above.

he built an electric locomotive, which he demonstrated on a 900-foot (274.3-meter) track. In 1881 he installed a regular train line in a suburb of Berlin.

Thereafter it all came in a rush. In the 1880s streetcar lines were electrified in many cities in the United States, Europe, and elsewhere, and by the 1890s most American cities had electric streetcars.

There were many types of streetcars, but most of them used an overhead electric line connected to the car by a pole. The wheel at the end of the pole traveled along the wire to make the electrical contact. It was known as a trolley. These "trolley cars," as they came to be called, quickly became the basic transportation for city dwellers going to work, to shop, and to baseball games and theaters. The famous Brooklyn Dodgers baseball team (now the Los Angeles Dodgers) initially got their name because Brooklyn was known as a city of trolley dodgers. The trolley car eventually faded from the American scene with the arrival of cars and buses, but they continue to be used in many European cities where narrow streets are less adaptable to modern buses.

This same period saw the beginnings of one of the most important social movements of the last hundred years in the United States—the growth of the suburbs. As the populations of cities exploded almost out of control, they became less desirable places to live in. There was crime, poverty, and overcrowding, which permitted the rapid spread of disease. People who could afford it—the relatively small but growing middle class—looked for better places to settle. They found them on the outskirts of the cities, where they could build houses surrounded by large lawns planted with trees, amid fresh air along clean streets.

But the breadwinners in these families, at the time usually the husbands, generally worked in the cities. There were then few automobiles. Soon inter-urban railway lines were built, which ran on electricity and reached into the suburbs. Inevitably, suburbs tended to grow along the inter-urban railway lines, which radiated outward from the central cities like the spokes of a wheel. Not until cheap automobiles were available would the spaces between the spokes fill in with more suburban towns and villages.

The new, powerful electric motor was also responsible for the development of another crucially important transport system, the subway. Coal-fired steam engines would have filled subway tunnels with smoke, which was not only dirty but dangerous to breathe. Electricity was clean and made it possible to move urban transportation routes underground.

The first subways were built in London in 1890. The London "tube" network is still one of the greatest in the world. In America the first subways were built in Boston in 1897. The New York system, now the country's largest, was started in 1904. Today it consists of 722 miles (1162 kilometers) of track. New York students ride to school along the same subway lines that their parents, grandparents, even great-grandparents did. Most big cities in the United States now have subways.

Today, of course, transportation fueled by electricity is part of everyday life. It is not just in use in the subways. Elevators, escalators, and moving walkways all run on electricity. Although steam locomotives are still used, millions of workers ride electric commuter trains every day. The electrical automobile is becoming practical as well and will probably be widely used in another twenty years.

By about 1900, then, the industrial world had become mostly electrified. Not every home had electricity, and horses were still pulling streetcars through cities. It would be a while before electricity came to the countryside. But even by 1900 it was clear that the world of the future would run on electricity. And a hundred years later we have no doubt that it is.

The story of electricity does not end with electric lights and electric trains. Electricity also revolutionized communications. At the same time that the electric bulb was being developed, inventors like Alexander Graham Bell, Guglielmo Marconi, Samuel Morse, Hermann Helmholtz, Heinrich Hertz, Nikola Tesla, and many others were developing the

ELECTRIC AUTOMOBILES ARE STILL MORE EXPENSIVE TO RUN THAN GAS-POWERED CARS. HOWEVER, FUTURE SHORTAGES OF OIL WILL ALMOST CERTAINLY MAKE ELECTRIC CARS ESSENTIAL. AMONG OTHER THINGS, THEY CREATE LESS AIR POLLUTION THAN GAS-POWERED MODELS. HERE, A WOMAN IN JAPAN RECHARGES HER ELECTRIC CAR.

telegraph, the telephone, the phonograph, and the wireless telegraph. Understanding of the electromagnetic spectrum grew rapidly, and by 1920 commercial radio was a reality in the United States. Television progressed more slowly, but was in use in a few homes in America in the 1940s and became widespread in the 1950s. Then came computers and a host of new electrical devices like transistors and semiconductors. The story of electricity, and its impact on the world, continues to be written.

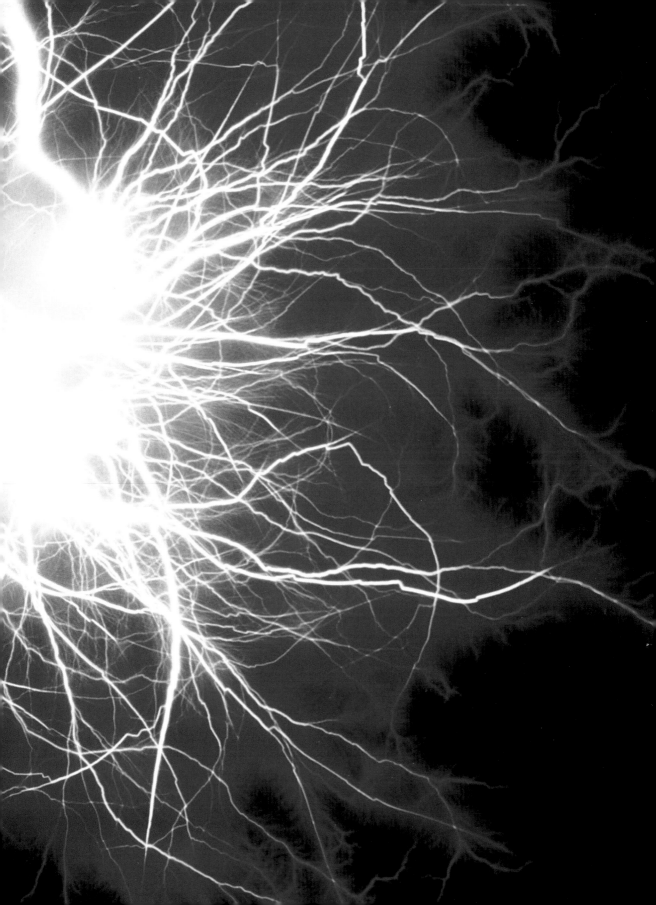

alternating current—An electrical current that reverses its direction of flow at regular intervals and has a magnitude that varies continuously.

amp—Short for ampere, the unit of measure used to express an electrical current's strength or rate of flow.

arc—A sustained luminous discharge of electricity across a gap in a circuit or between electrodes.

conduction—The ability to transmit or carry an electrical current.

direct current—An electrical current that flows continuously in one direction.

dynamo—A generator, a device that creates electrical power.

electron—A negatively charged particle that is a component of atoms.

field—A region or space in which a given effect, such as magnetism, exists or operates.

filament—A thread, wire, or other piece of thin flexible material made incandescent by the flow of electrical current.

hypothesis—A theory or supposition that is tested and either proved or disproved.

incandescence—The release or emission of radiation that makes a heated body visible.

kilowatt hour—A unit of energy with which one kilowatt of power is expended for one hour. An appliance rated at 1,000 watts and run for an hour will consume one kilowatt hour of electricity.

ohm—A unit of electrical resistance defined as the resistance of a circuit in which a force of one volt maintains a current flow of one ampere.

permanent magnet—A material that retains its magnetism independent of an outside magnetizing force.

quantify—To determine or measure the quantity of.

repel—To exert a force, to drive something away; the opposite of *attract.*

resistance—A measure of the opposition a conducting material gives to electrical current flow, a quantity expressed in ohms.

torsion balance—A device that can measure the force required to twist and bend wires, rods, or other similar materials.

transformer—An electromagnetic device used to change the voltage in an alternating-current electrical circuit.

volt—A unit used to measure the force that drives an electrical current; the electrical potential needed to produce one ampere of current through a conductor with a resistance of one ohm.

voltaic pile—A stack of metallic disks, interlaced with an acid-soaked buffering agent, capable of producing an electrical current.

walking beam—A component of early motors that powered machinery by moving up and down in a seesaw motion, pulled by electromagnets attached to each end of the beam.

wattage—Amount of electrical power, expressed in watts.

600 B.C.E.
Greek philosopher Thales first describes static electricity, when he charges a piece of amber by rubbing it.

1550 C.E.
Jerome Cardan adds to the growing knowledge of lodestone, amber, and magnetism.

1600
William Gilbert first coins the term *electrics*. His influential work *De Magnete* is published.

1660
Otto von Guericke invents a machine that produces static electricity.

1729
Stephen Gray conducts experiments on the conductive properties of electricity.

1733

Charles Dufay concludes there are two forms of electrical charge, which he describes as resinous and vitreous, or positive and negative.

1745

E. G. von Kleist experiments with electrical charges and discovers that electricity can be controlled. Pieter van Musschenbroek invents the first electrical capacitor, the Leyden jar.

1752

Benjamin Franklin invents the lightning rod and demonstrates that lightning is a form of electricity.

1780–1791

Luigi Galvani demonstrates the electrical basis of nerve impulses by moving the muscles of frogs with sparks from an electrostatic machine.

1785

Charles Coulomb develops a machine that can measure electrical force.

1800

Alessandro Volta publishes his paper detailing the electric battery, which he most likely first developed in 1792.

1819

Hans Christian Oersted confirms the relationship between electricity and magnetism when he observes a compass needle move when it is placed near an electrical source.

1820

André-Marie Ampère discovers that coiled wires become magnetized when a current is passed through them.
François Arago develops a simple electromagnet.

1821

Michael Faraday proposes the concept of the field and develops the principles behind the electric motor.

1825–1827

Georg Simon Ohm begins studying the flow of current through conductors. He proposes his law involving conduction and resistance.

1831–1845

Michael Faraday builds the first electric generator. He continues his pioneering work exploring the induction, generation, and transmission of electromagnetism.

1831

Joseph Henry produces an electromagnet capable of lifting a ton and begins to develop a notion of the electromagnetic spectrum.

1834

Thomas Davenport develops his powerful walking-beam motor.

1858

Arc lighting is first used in England's South Foreland Lighthouse.

1873

James Clerk Maxwell works out formulas for electric and magnetic fields that show how the lines of force in such fields behave.

1878

Joseph Swan produces the first workable lightbulb.

1879

Thomas Edison creates a lightbulb with a carbonized thread filament and demonstrates the incandescent lamp.

1882
Thomas Edison's Pearl Street power station in New York City goes into operation.

1888
Nikola Tesla patents his AC motor.

1893
George Westinghouse demonstrates his AC lighting system at the World's Columbia Exhibition in Chicago.

1901
The electric vacuum cleaner and washing machine are invented.

1902
The first air conditioner appears.

1913
The electric refrigerator is developed.

1947
The transistor is invented.

1991
Philips invents a lightbulb that uses magnetic induction and lasts 60,000 hours.

http://inventors.about.com/library/inventors/bllight.htm
This site offers an overview of the history of lightbulbs, lighting, and lamps. It also provides links to biographies of key figures, a time line, and various topics in the history of electricity and lighting.

http://www.ideafinder.com/history/inventions/story074.htm
This Web page focuses on the development of the lightbulb as seen mostly through the lens of Thomas Edison's contributions. It also offers links to a general history of electricity and more in-depth coverage of the life of Edison.

http://www.eei.org/industry_issues/industry_overview_and_statistics/history/
The Edison Electric Institute hosts this site detailing the history of the electric-power industry as well as providing links to a time line, information on Edison's development of the lightbulb, and an article discussing the differences between alternating and direct current.

http://www.ideafinder.com/history/inventions/story066.htm
This page offers a glimpse at the history of the electric battery as well as a link to a profile of inventor Alessandro Volta.

http://maxwell.byu.edu/~spencerr/phys442/node4.html
This page offers a detailed time line of milestones in electrical history.

http://inventors.about.com/library/inventors/blelectric3.htm

This related site discusses the history of electromagnetism and the growing knowledge of magnetic fields. Browsers are also offered a Time Line of Electromagnetism and an opportunity to replicate Hans Christian Oersted's groundbreaking experiment, using a compass, a wire, and a battery.

http://www.ieee-virtual-museum.org/

This site, part of the Institute of Electrical and Electronics Engineers (IEEE) Virtual Museum, offers a brief history of electricity and its applications. It features exhibits such as Socket to Me and Let's Get Small: The Shrinking World of Microelectronics.

http://inventors.about.com/library/inventors/blelectric.htm

A valuable resource, the site offers articles on electronics, electrical theory as well as links to biographies of electrical scientists, a time line, a history of electromagnetism, and additional information on dynamos and electrostatic devices.

http://library.thinkquest.org/6064/

This site lives up to its claim of offering the Shocking Truth about Electricity. It offers information about power sources, power failures, the history of electricity, and other helpful links.

http://www.infoplease.com/ce6/sci/A0857938.html

In addition to a brief overview of the early history of electricity, the site offers links that help explain the technical and scientific side of electronics, including information on the properties of electric charges, charges at rest, and charges in motion.

http://www.code-electrical.com/historyofelectricity.html
A brief overview of the major figures in the history of electricity, the site also offers links detailing possible careers in the electrical field.

BOOKS

FOR OLDER READERS
Collins, Theresa M. *Thomas A. Edison and Modern America*. New York: Bedford/Saint Martin's, 2002.

Davis, L. J. *Fleet Fire: Thomas Edison and the Pioneers of the Electric Revolution*. New York: Arcade, 2003.

Jonnes, Jill. *Empires of Light: Edison, Tesla, Westinghouse, and the Race to Electrify the World*. New York: Random House, 2003.

FOR YOUNGER READERS
Adair, Gene. *Thomas Alva Edison: Inventing the Electric Age*. Oxford Portraits in Science series. New York: Oxford University Press, 1997.

Ardley, Neil. *Electricity*. Way It Works series. New York: Simon and Schuster Childrens, 1999.

Dolan, Ellen M. *Thomas Alva Edison: Inventor*. Historical American Biographies series. Berkeley Heights, NJ: Enslow, 1998.

Dommermuth-Costa, Carol. *Nikola Tesla: A Spark of Genius*. Lerner Biographies series. Minneapolis, MN: Lerner, 1994.

Gardner, Robert. *Science Projects about Electricity and Magnetism*. Berkeley Heights, NJ: Enslow, 1994.

Pollard, Michael. *The Light Bulb and How It Changed the World*. New York: Facts on File, 1995.

Ravage, Barbara. *George Westinghouse: A Genius for Inventions*. Innovative Minds series. Austin, TX: Raintree, 1997.

Stwertka, Albert. *Superconductors: The Irresistible Future*. Danbury, CT: Scholastic Library, 1991.

Wallace, Joseph. *Light Bulbs*. Turning Point Inventions series. New York: Atheneum Books for Young Readers, 1999.

Page numbers for illustrations are in **boldface**.

About the Author

James Lincoln Collier has written books for both adults and students on many subjects, among them the prizewinning novel *My Brother Sam Is Dead.* Many of these books, both fiction and nonfiction, have historical themes, including the highly acclaimed Marshall Cavendish Benchmark series the Drama of American History, which he wrote with Christopher Collier.